The Midnight Trail ~

A Christmas story
by Phil Forder and Peter Oram
with Illustrations by Phil Forder

STARBORN BOOKS

The Midnight Trail ~

First published 1995
by STARBORN BOOKS

Copyright Starborn Books © 1995

ISBN 1 899530 02 9

British Library Cataloguing in Publication Data

A catalogue record for this book is available from the British Library.

STARBORN BOOKS
3 Union Terrace, St. Dogmaels, Cardigan, Dyfed. SA43 3LA.

Printed by E. L. Jones & Son, Cardigan, Dyfed.

I

THE COW'S TALE

Winter. The byre is snug and warm.
Outside, the bleak and blistering storm
with sleet and snow in buffeting squalls
rattles the roof and beats the walls.

Though summer's days are far away
I taste their fragrance in the hay
and dream of summers yet to come,
of flowery meadows' drowsy hum.

Every morning, every night
I give my milk, rich, creamy white
to that fair maid who cares for me :
no other is as good as she !

Hark ! Here she comes - the bucket rings,
and as she milks she sweetly sings.

Now she is done. But look, oh look !
- she takes my halter from the hook
and lays it soft around my head
and gently says : "There's nought to dread !"

Alas, alas ! I'm to be sold -
and that in winter bleak and cold -
and never more my mistress sweet
shall groom my coat and clean my feet !

So poor she is she must me sell ...
Ah dearest mistress mine, farewell !

II

THE DONKEY'S TALE

Jobs, jobs and more jobs to be done -
indeed, my life's a busy one !
Whatever in the house may lack
I fetch in baskets on my back :

some days it's water from the spring,
some days the fireplace logs I bring ;
on Wednesdays we to market go -
no load's too much for me, you know !

My master he is good and kind :
a better man you scarce would find ;
he is a carpenter by trade -
and *I* deliver what he's made :

        windows, tables, chairs - or toys
        for lucky little girls and boys.

See - mistress Mary comes this way !
What is to be my task today ?
... She leaves my baskets on the rack
and lifts ... a *saddle* on my back !

"This is to be a special day,"
she says, "for we must go away
and journey far across the land
- and *you* shall carry me, my friend ..."

"Me ? Carry you ? - With all my heart !
Oh, what an honour ! - When can we start ?"

III

THE JOURNEY

"Well, brother ass, this worries me :
what can our journey's purpose be ?
As if to Nazareth we set out,
then at the crossroads turned about

and headed out across the land ...
I truly do not understand.
All morning long we plodded on
through towns and hamlets one by one,

until the sun stood at its height.
We briefly paused to have a bite,
then trotted on o'er hill and dale.
Now sun has set and, great and pale,

        the moon has sailed into the sky :
        I'm tired. Where do we go ? And why ?"

"Oh, sister cow, nor do I know
whither on journey far we go.
Yet in my master full I trust :
if go he tells us, go we must -

and though we travel day and night
I bear my load with quiet delight.
Be silent now, the hour is late
and I need peace to concentrate

      or else I'll bump from side to side :
      sweet Mary must in comfort ride."

IV

THE CAT'S TALE

Miaow ! What a busy day it's been -
so many folk I've never seen !
Our inn has never been so packed :
from floor to roof there's people stacked.

Why do they come, *I'd* like to know,
in winter too, with all this snow ?
All beds are taken, every one
- and all my favourite places gone.

Me, I stalked off into town
and stayed out till the sun went down.
When I returned - well, that was that :
not even room to swing a cat !

At last I curled up on a heap
of snoring folk, and fell asleep.

Upon the hour of midnight's stroke
I know not why, but I awoke.
All around me folk slept tight -
but *what* was that pale, gleaming light

that shone in through the window there ?
- A wondrous maid beyond compare
with radiant features did I see !
She peered inside, but then, since she

could spy no little space to stay
she sighed, and went upon her way.

V

THE GOOSE'S TALE

My master's not a pleasant type :
day in day out you hear him gripe.
He kicks me out the way, with words
that quite disturb us decent birds.

Yet when today he passed me by
there was a sparkle in his eye :
"My dear", he cried and poked my rump,
"my dear, you're looking good and plump !"

Now what this meant, alas I knew :
he's planning up a tasty stew ...
the fire's all ready in the grate -
I'll end up on the dinner plate !

Not me ! I'm off ! I'm out the door
to hide beneath the barnyard straw ...

All evening long I heard him curse :
"That goose - I'll wring her neck and worse !"
He's in a foul mood, I can tell ...
but who's *this* ringing at the bell ?

- A dear old man, a gentle maid -
he won't take *them* in, I'm afraid !
"Be off, the pair of you !" he roars,
"I don't let beggars in my doors !"

They can't believe their sorry plight
and trudge back into frosty night ...

VI

THE GOAT'S TALE

I have a cosy little stall
set right against the city wall ;
in front you'll find my master's inn,
behind, the desolate moors begin.

Just after sunset, every day,
my master milks me, brings me hay,
and calls me "little sweetie pie !"
and chats about the day gone by.

Last night he told me, "mark my words :
full house tomorrow - there are herds
of folk a-coming into town
to pay old Caesar's tribute down."

Today has proved him right, for sure :
the inn is bursting at the door.

This night the snow fell white and deep,
but I was snug and half asleep
when, look ! - a lantern bobbing bright !
My master up so late at night ?

He led an old man and his spouse :
they trudged on past my little house ;
he showed the way across the snow -
and off they went ... where did they go

      all in the night so cold and deep ?
      For wondering I could not sleep ...

VII

THE TALE OF THE MICE

Furtive and secretive, scampering, scurrying,
little feet pattering, busily hurrying
hither and thither, then gone in a trice ...
- we are the mice !

From dawn until dusk in the fields we run,
and though the harvest has long been done,
our sharp little eyes find many a grain
and carry it back to our castle again.

Our castle ? To others it may be a shed
with a leaky and tumbledown roof overhead
but to us it's home - and a mansion at that,
and a haven of safety from buzzard and cat,

and there, every evening, our friends come to visit :
we sing until sunrise with voices exquisite.

One night while expecting arrival of kin,
the door it creaked open - and who should come in
but a fair gentle maid with an ass at her side
and a wizened old man with a cow : this they tied

with a rope to a rickety post in our shed,
then, spreading some straw on the floor for a bed,
they lay down and huddled together to sleep,
while we mousefolk in utter amazement did peep

as, in spite of the snow and the icy-cold air,
they whispered in thanks, ere they slept, a soft prayer.

VIII

THE ROBINS' TALE

When summer is over and winter starts
the swallow to warmer lands departs,
yet we, the robins, we do not go -
we stay to brave the ice and snow.

When winds blow bitter and rivers freeze
we hide in the ivy-encircled trees
or in rocky crannies we huddle together,
little heads tucked into puffed-up feather.

If even for that it blows too cold,
there's a tumbledown stable we know of old :
there in the hay it is sheltered and warm,
there it is silent, in spite of the storm

- except for the mice and their finely-tuned chorus,
but we don't mind them, and they mostly ignore us.

One blizzardy night, what a sight met our eyes :
from the rafters we saw to our utter surprise
how a weary old man and a shivering maid
a tangle of straw for a fire had laid.

No matter how hard the poor maid blew,
the spark would not catch on the straw wet through -
so we fluttered on down and our wings we beat
till the flames blazed brightly and gave them heat.

Then this radiant maiden us softly addressed :
"As winter's birds may you ever be blessed !"

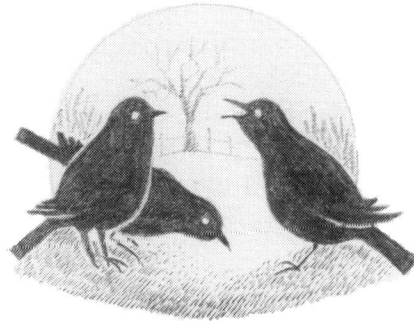

IX

THE TALE OF THE SHEEP

We are the woolly ones. Mountain and moor
are our domain. Though the land is poor
we always find something to nibble - small shoots,
or wisps of grass and occasional roots.

When evening comes we gather together
and, huddled up close to be safe from the weather,
we gaze at the stars as they pass through the skies
and discuss in a manner incredibly wise

the ways of the world, and of beasts and men.
For hours we earnestly argue, and then
we are finally silent, and patiently wait
for the coming of morning, and ruminate.

        Thus all the night long we a vigil keep,
        and watch over our shepherds while they are asleep.

But one dark night as on snow we lay
- twas the darkest hour and distant the day -
we had sensed a great wonder and now it was certain :
the heavens drew back their velvet curtain

and earth was bathed in an ocean of light,
as a thousand angels shimmering bright
filled all of the skies with celestial singing -
what tidings of joy to the world they were bringing !

Our shepherds lay sleeping - no move did they make :
though we bleated and bleated, they would not awake.

X

THE LAMB'S TALE

One misty morning I was born :
the wind it howled with voice forlorn.
A shepherd found me all alone
and cold and frozen to the bone.

He took me to his little hut,
made sure the door was tightly shut
against the wild and wintry storm,
and lit a fire to make me warm.

He gave me milk : in strength I grew
till, when a month had passed or two,
he took me from my straw-filled box
and led me back among the flocks

with whom I dwell now. All the same
I come whene'er he calls my name.

One morning with the rising sun
I heard him cry, "Come, Snowflake - run !
To Bethlem swiftly we must go !"
He washed me till I shone like snow

and, lifting me upon his back,
set off along the moorland track.
At last I spied a stable poor :
we entered through the creaking door -

and oh, the wonder ! Oh, the light !
Never shall I forget that sight !

XI

TO THE STABLE

In Bethlem Town all are asleep,
but through the snow soft, white and deep
that over all the country lays
three creatures make their separate ways.

To sleep they could no longer bear
once they had seen that gentle pair
in vain seek shelter for the night
then trudge in sadness out of sight.

And thus each slowly onward moves :
the first one trots on cloven hooves ;
on velvet paws the second springs ;
with webbed feet walks the third, its wings

      out-stretched to beat away the sleet.
      Out on the moors, these creatures meet.

They question, find their goal is one -
together then they journey on,
stumbling, falling in the snow.
Says goat, "I see a distant glow."

They hasten onward. Says the cat,
"I see a stable. Surely that
can't be the place !" Says goose, "Indeed,
it seems that's where the footprints lead !"

With tails a-wag they race ahead
and reach at last the humble shed.

XII

IN THE STABLE

Though through the door they dared not tread,
the three a window found instead :
the cat sprang up onto the ledge,
the goat laid forefeet on the edge

and pressed her nose against the pane.
The goose her long white neck did crane
to pluck off cobwebs with her beak.
They peered inside - oh, none dared speak !

... for there they saw a wondrous sight :
a tiny child, all bathed in light,
lay smiling on his mother's knee
while angels chorussed joyfully.

> Each creature's heart leapt too with joy
> to see the little heavenly boy.

Now kind old Joseph makes his way
towards the door, to gently say,
"Come in, good creatures, come inside !"
The creaking door he opens wide -

and shyly enter whiskered puss
and bearded goat and waddling goose.
Sweet Mary beckons to the three
to come and sit close by her knee.

The Christ Child strokes the cat's soft fur
and laughs with joy to hear him purr.

Epilogue :

THE GIFTS

And so upon the straw-strewn ground
these humble creatures gathered round.
Before at daybreak to depart
each deeply searched within its heart

to find a gift to offer there,
full worthy of that child most rare.
The donkey said, "The breadth and length
of my strong back shall bring you strength."

The cow said, "Since my milk is sweet
I bring you sweetness." "Since our feet
are swift and light," the mousefolk said,
"we bring you speed for ways ahead."

"Since I the gentlest creature am,
I bring you meekness," said the lamb.

Then spoke the cat : "My silent ways
shall comfort you in darker days."
Said goose, "You ne'er shall water fear."
The goat gave power to persevere.

The robins gave their gift of flight
and skill of balance. In delight
the Christ Child did accept each gift,
did tiny hands in blessing lift -

a blessing that each creature bore
deep in its heart for evermore.

A Note about this book

The principal illustrations of *The Midnight Trail* had their origin in a wish to deepen the Christmas experience of 1994. Each was drawn in turn on one of the twelve Holy Nights, and out of these the story unfurled. In an age of ever-increasing materialism it is hoped that this little book may inspire and delight young and old alike, and help to reaffirm the Christ in Christmas.

Phil Forder, Rhydwilym 1995

The story was conceived and shaped by Phil Forder, and set into its verse form by Peter Oram.

If you have enjoyed this book you may be interested in some other titles published by Starborn Books :

SEVEN STARS OF GOLD :
>A collection of poems for children written by Peter Oram and illustrated by Phil Forder. ISBN 1 899530 01 0. Price £5.00

PETER'S BOOK OF ROUNDS :
>A collection of rounds and canons, composed by Peter Oram and illustrated by Phil Forder. ISBN 1 899530 00 2. Price : £5.00

Both books are obtainable through your local bookshop, or else may be ordered direct from the address on the reverse of the title page of this book.

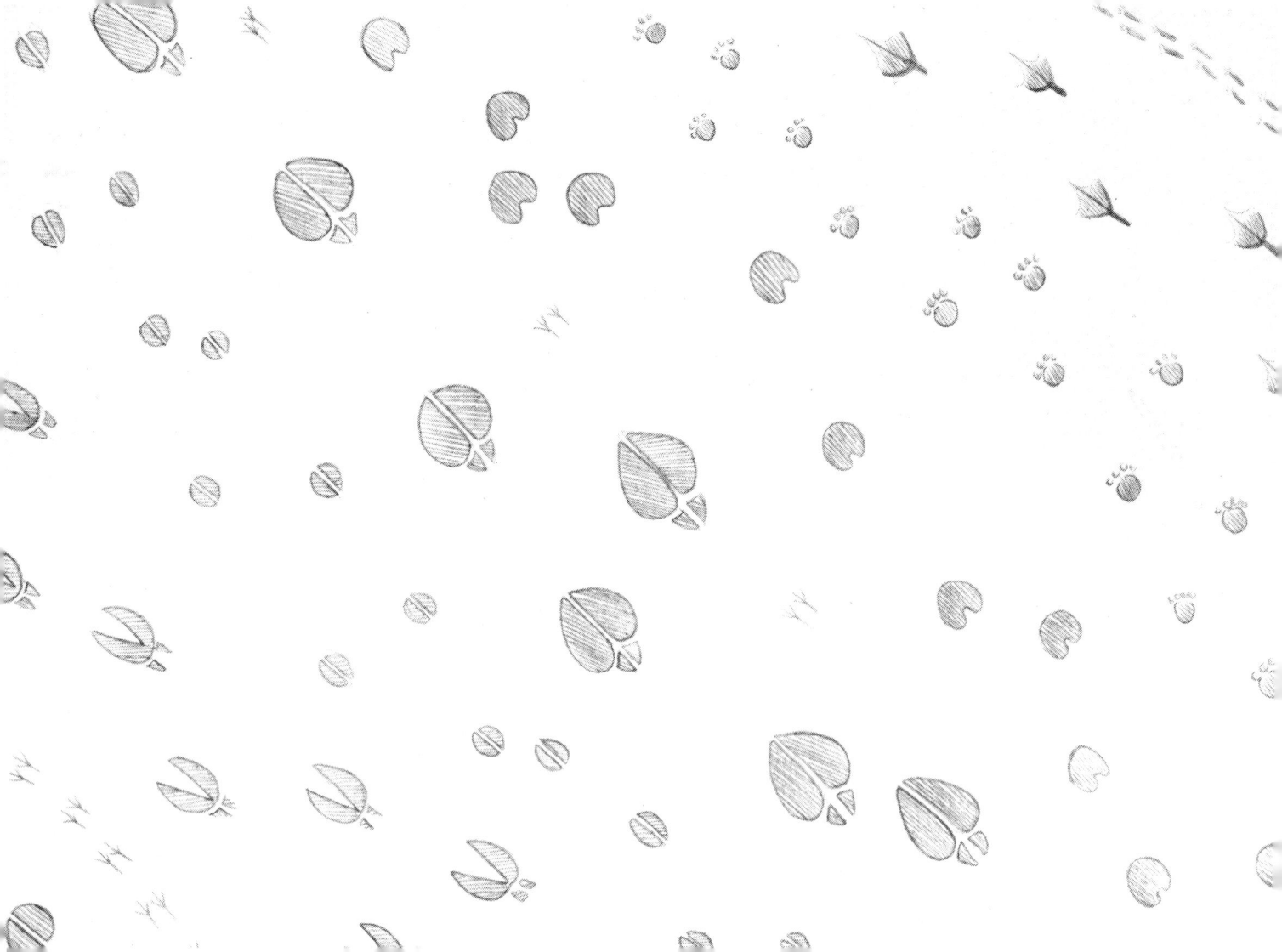